MAD LIBS®

HOME FROM SCHOOL
MAD LIBS

by Kim Ostrow

MAD LIBS
An Imprint of Penguin Random House LLC, New York

Concept created by Roger Price & Leonard Stern

Cover illustration by Scott Brooks

Published by Mad Libs,
an imprint of Penguin Random House LLC, New York.
Printed in the USA.

Visit us online at www.penguinrandomhouse.com.

ISBN 9780593226209
1 3 5 7 9 10 8 6 4 2
COMR

MAD LIBS

INSTRUCTIONS

MAD LIBS® is a game for people who don't like games!
It can be played by one, two, three, four, or forty.

● RIDICULOUSLY SIMPLE DIRECTIONS

In this tablet you will find stories containing blank spaces where words
are left out. One player, the READER, selects one of these stories. The
READER does not tell anyone what the story is about. Instead, he/she asks
the other players, the WRITERS, to give him/her words. These words are
used to fill in the blank spaces in the story.

● TO PLAY

The READER asks each WRITER in turn to call out a word—an adjective or
a noun or whatever the space calls for—and uses them to fill in the blank
spaces in the story. The result is a MAD LIBS® game.

When the READER then reads the completed MAD LIBS® game to the other
players, they will discover that they have written a story that is fantastic,
screamingly funny, shocking, silly, crazy, or just plain dumb—depending
upon which words each WRITER called out.

● EXAMPLE (*Before* and *After*)

"_____!" he said _____
           EXCLAMATION   ADVERB

as he jumped into his convertible _____ and
                                              NOUN

drove off with his _____ wife.
                            ADJECTIVE

"_____OUCH_____!" he said _____HAPPILY_____
        EXCLAMATION   ADVERB

as he jumped into his convertible _____CAT_____ and
                                          NOUN

drove off with his _____BRAVE_____ wife.
                          ADJECTIVE

In case you have forgotten what adjectives, adverbs, nouns, and verbs are, here is a quick review:

An ADJECTIVE describes something or somebody. *Lumpy, soft, ugly, messy,* and *short* are adjectives.

An ADVERB tells how something is done. It modifies a verb and usually ends in "ly." *Modestly, stupidly, greedily,* and *carefully* are adverbs.

A NOUN is the name of a person, place, or thing. *Sidewalk, umbrella, bridle, bathtub,* and *nose* are nouns.

A VERB is an action word. *Run, pitch, jump,* and *swim* are verbs. Put the verbs in past tense if the directions say PAST TENSE. *Ran, pitched, jumped,* and *swam* are verbs in the past tense.

When we ask for A PLACE, we mean any sort of place: a country or city (*Spain, Cleveland*) or a room (*bathroom, kitchen*).

An EXCLAMATION or SILLY WORD is any sort of funny sound, gasp, grunt, or outcry, like *Wow!, Ouch!, Whomp!, Ick!,* and *Gadzooks!*

When we ask for specific words, like a NUMBER, a COLOR, an ANIMAL, or a PART OF THE BODY, we mean a word that is one of those things, like *seven, blue, horse,* or *head.*

When we ask for a PLURAL, it means more than one. For example, *cat* pluralized is *cats.*

MAD LIBS® is fun to play with friends, but you can also play it by yourself! To begin with, DO NOT look at the story on the page below. Fill in the blanks on this page with the words called for. Then, using the words you have selected, fill in the blank spaces in the story.

Now you've created your own hilarious MAD LIBS® game!

SNOW DAY

PERSON IN ROOM _____

PLURAL NOUN _____

ARTICLE OF CLOTHING _____

VERB _____

ADJECTIVE _____

A PLACE _____

TYPE OF LIQUID _____

NUMBER _____

VERB ENDING IN "ING" _____

ADJECTIVE _____

NOUN _____

NOUN _____

NUMBER _____

PLURAL NOUN _____

ADJECTIVE _____

VERB ENDING IN "ING" _____

TYPE OF LIQUID _____

ADJECTIVE _____

MAD LIBS®

SNOW DAY

And now a weather report from meteorologist _____ . . .
<u>PERSON IN ROOM</u>

"Good morning, _____! Better put on your warmest
<u>PLURAL NOUN</u>

_____ if you're planning to _____ outside
<u>ARTICLE OF CLOTHING</u>   <u>VERB</u>

today—looks like it is going to be a/an _____ one! A storm
<u>ADJECTIVE</u>

from (the) _____ is bringing a mix of sleet and freezing
<u>A PLACE</u>

_____ . We can expect more than _____ feet of snow
<u>TYPE OF LIQUID</u>   <u>NUMBER</u>

later in the day, _____ off after midnight. Skies will
<u>VERB ENDING IN "ING"</u>

remain _____ and the _____-chill will make it feel
<u>ADJECTIVE</u>   <u>NOUN</u>

as cold as a/an _____ out there. Tonight, temperatures will
<u>NOUN</u>

drop to _____ below zero, making the _____
<u>NUMBER</u>   <u>PLURAL NOUN</u>

icy, and causing _____ conditions for drivers. For all the
<u>ADJECTIVE</u>

kids out there, school buses aren't _____ today,
<u>VERB ENDING IN "ING"</u>

so you know what that means: Time to warm up a mug of hot

_____ . It's our first _____ snow day of the
<u>TYPE OF LIQUID</u>   <u>ADJECTIVE</u>

season!"

MAD LIBS® is fun to play with friends, but you can also play it by yourself! To begin with, DO NOT look at the story on the page below. Fill in the blanks on this page with the words called for. Then, using the words you have selected, fill in the blank spaces in the story.

Now you've created your own hilarious MAD LIBS® game!

SNOW SCHEDULE

PART OF THE BODY _____

VERB _____

NOUN _____

PLURAL NOUN _____

ADJECTIVE _____

NUMBER _____

TYPE OF CONTAINER _____

TYPE OF FOOD _____

PLURAL NOUN _____

VERB _____

TYPE OF BUILDING _____

NUMBER _____

PLURAL NOUN _____

ADJECTIVE _____

NOUN _____

ADJECTIVE _____

VERB _____

VERB _____

MAD LIBS®

SNOW SCHEDULE

There's plenty you can do to keep your _____

PART OF THE BODY

occupied when you're home from school. Here are some things you can

_____ the next time you have a snow day. First, read your

VERB

favorite _____ from the library or magazines about

NOUN

_____ , or even play a/an _____ Libs—they're

PLURAL NOUN   ADJECTIVE

fun and can keep you entertained for over _____ hours! Next,

NUMBER

get some healthy food from inside the _____ , like

TYPE OF CONTAINER

_____ soup or scrambled _____ and toast. Good

TYPE OF FOOD   PLURAL NOUN

food makes you _____ faster. And who doesn't love building

VERB

a/an _____ in their bedroom? All you need are

TYPE OF BUILDING

_____ pillows and quilted _____ . You'll be safe

NUMBER   PLURAL NOUN

and _____ under there. Of course, you can always play a

ADJECTIVE

board _____ if you want. They're a little _____ to

NOUN   ADJECTIVE

_____ by yourself, but look at it this way—at least you'll

VERB

always _____ !

VERB

MAD LIBS® is fun to play with friends, but you can also play it by yourself! To begin with, DO NOT look at the story on the page below. Fill in the blanks on this page with the words called for. Then, using the words you have selected, fill in the blank spaces in the story.

Now you've created your own hilarious MAD LIBS® game!

HUNGER GAME

VERB _____

ADJECTIVE _____

VERB _____

SOMETHING ALIVE _____

NOUN _____

ADJECTIVE _____

PERSON IN ROOM _____

VERB _____

TYPE OF FOOD _____

ADJECTIVE _____

NOUN _____

VERB _____

NUMBER _____

EXCLAMATION _____

NOUN _____

A PLACE _____

ADJECTIVE _____

VERB _____

NOUN _____

MAD LIBS®

HUNGER GAME

When hunger strikes, I like to _____ a delicious and
                                    VERB

_____ snack. Some of my favorite things to _____ are
  ADJECTIVE   VERB

sandwiches. A/An _____ wrap, grilled cheese, or peanut
                    SOMETHING ALIVE

butter and _____ sandwich are all _____ choices,
              NOUN   ADJECTIVE

but the best one is a little creation I like to call the _____
                                                          PERSON IN ROOM

Surprise. Here's how to make it! First, you _____ the bread
                                                 VERB

with mustard. Next, pile on slices of _____—use a lot, don't
                                        TYPE OF FOOD

be _____! Feel free to add _____ cheese or ketchup.
     ADJECTIVE   NOUN

_____ on _____ pickles. _____! The most
     VERB   NUMBER   EXCLAMATION

important ingredient is the sour cream and _____ potato
                                                NOUN

chips. Place the chips inside the sandwich for a flavor that's out of this

_____ . Now you've made the _____ snack. And
  A PLACE   ADJECTIVE

don't worry, no one else will _____ it, so you won't have to
                                  VERB

share with your _____!
                    NOUN

MAD LIBS® is fun to play with friends, but you can also play it by yourself! To begin with, DO NOT look at the story on the page below. Fill in the blanks on this page with the words called for. Then, using the words you have selected, fill in the blank spaces in the story.

Now you've created your own hilarious MAD LIBS® game!

TEXT ME!

PERSON IN ROOM _____

EXCLAMATION _____

NOUN _____

VERB ENDING IN "ING" _____

NOUN _____

VERB (PAST TENSE) _____

TYPE OF BUILDING _____

EXCLAMATION _____

VERB ENDING IN "ING" _____

CELEBRITY _____

VERB ENDING IN "ING" _____

ANIMAL _____

ADJECTIVE _____

VERB ENDING IN "ING" _____

TYPE OF FOOD _____

ADJECTIVE _____

ADVERB _____

NOUN _____

MAD LIBS®

TEXT ME!

Friend 1: Hey, _____ ! Are you home rn?
<u>PERSON IN ROOM</u>

Friend 2: _____ ! We have a/an _____ day, so I'm
<u>EXCLAMATION</u>   <u>NOUN</u>

just _____ a/an _____ game. You?
<u>VERB ENDING IN "ING"</u>   <u>NOUN</u>

Friend 1: Our school is _____, too. When I heard
<u>VERB (PAST TENSE)</u>

we had no _____ today, I screamed, "_____!"
<u>TYPE OF BUILDING</u>   <u>EXCLAMATION</u>

Now I'm _____ with _____ . jk. I'm home
<u>VERB ENDING IN "ING"</u>   <u>CELEBRITY</u>

_____ with my _____ .
<u>VERB ENDING IN "ING"</u>   <u>ANIMAL</u>

Friend 2: Oh, that's _____ . ☺ Hang on, my mom is
<u>ADJECTIVE</u>

_____ . brb.
<u>VERB ENDING IN "ING"</u>

Friend 2: I'm back! She made me some _____ . Snow days are
<u>TYPE OF FOOD</u>

so _____!
<u>ADJECTIVE</u>

Friend 1: I _____ agree. I hope we keep having
<u>ADVERB</u>

_____ -storms until graduation!
<u>NOUN</u>

MAD LIBS® is fun to play with friends, but you can also play it by yourself! To begin with, DO NOT look at the story on the page below. Fill in the blanks on this page with the words called for. Then, using the words you have selected, fill in the blank spaces in the story.

Now you've created your own hilarious MAD LIBS® game!

SNOW-DAY DITTY

VERB (PAST TENSE) _____

PLURAL NOUN _____

PART OF THE BODY (PLURAL) _____

VERB ENDING IN "ING" _____

ADVERB _____

VERB (PAST TENSE) _____

NOUN _____

VERB ENDING IN "ING" _____

NOUN _____

PLURAL NOUN _____

VERB (PAST TENSE) _____

EXCLAMATION _____

ADJECTIVE _____

MAD LIBS®

SNOW-DAY DITTY

Before I _____ into bed,
VERB (PAST TENSE)

I pulled the _____ down low.
PLURAL NOUN

Then I closed my _____ ,
PART OF THE BODY (PLURAL)

_____ it would snow.
VERB ENDING IN "ING"

And while I slept _____ ,
ADVERB

all _____ into my bed,
VERB (PAST TENSE)

I had dreams of _____-ball fights
NOUN

_____ in my head.
VERB ENDING IN "ING"

The next _____ , I woke up
NOUN

and yanked open the _____ right away.
PLURAL NOUN

I saw it had _____ all night,
VERB (PAST TENSE)

_____ ! It's a/an _____ day!
EXCLAMATION   ADJECTIVE

MAD LIBS® is fun to play with friends, but you can also play it by yourself! To begin with, DO NOT look at the story on the page below. Fill in the blanks on this page with the words called for. Then, using the words you have selected, fill in the blank spaces in the story.

Now you've created your own hilarious MAD LIBS® game!

SPA DAY

ADVERB _____

VERB _____

PLURAL NOUN _____

TYPE OF FOOD (PLURAL) _____

PART OF THE BODY (PLURAL) _____

ADJECTIVE _____

NUMBER _____

PART OF THE BODY _____

TYPE OF FOOD (PLURAL) _____

ADJECTIVE _____

VERB _____

NUMBER _____

ADJECTIVE _____

TYPE OF LIQUID _____

VERB _____

ANIMAL _____

VERB ENDING IN "ING" _____

VERB _____

MAD LIBS®

SPA DAY

You know what I _____ do when I'm stuck inside my house
                    ADVERB

on a snow day? I turn it into a spa day. It's always a fun way to

_____ the time. I start in the kitchen by gathering fruits and
     VERB

_____ . Then, I put sliced _____ on my
  PLURAL NOUN   TYPE OF FOOD (PLURAL)

_____ to relax! Just make sure you don't use a/an
PART OF THE BODY (PLURAL)

_____ pepper by mistake. I've made that mistake _____
   ADJECTIVE   NUMBER

too many times. A/An exfoliating _____ mask is
                                  PART OF THE BODY

another important part of any spa day. I like to mix oatmeal and

_____ until they form a/an _____ paste.
TYPE OF FOOD (PLURAL)   ADJECTIVE

Then you _____ the mixture all over your face and leave it on
            VERB

for _____ minutes. When the mask gets really _____ ,
       NUMBER   ADJECTIVE

wash it off with warm _____ . I guarantee you're going to
                       TYPE OF LIQUID

_____ great! But make sure you avoid going near the family
     VERB

_____ when you have your mask on. Our dog could not stop
   ANIMAL

_____ my face! Live and _____ !
VERB ENDING IN "ING"   VERB

MAD LIBS® is fun to play with friends, but you can also play it by yourself! To begin with, DO NOT look at the story on the page below. Fill in the blanks on this page with the words called for. Then, using the words you have selected, fill in the blank spaces in the story.

Now you've created your own hilarious MAD LIBS® game!

CLASS PET

SILLY WORD _____

ANIMAL _____

ADJECTIVE _____

TYPE OF FOOD _____

TYPE OF CONTAINER _____

VERB _____

ADJECTIVE _____

EXCLAMATION _____

ADJECTIVE _____

VEHICLE _____

VERB ENDING IN "ING" _____

SOMETHING ALIVE _____

NOUN _____

A PLACE _____

TYPE OF BUILDING _____

ADVERB _____

SAME SILLY WORD _____

NOUN _____

MAD LIBS®

CLASS PET

Yesterday, I got to bring home our class pet, _____ the
SILLY WORD
_____. She's supposed to be pretty _____ to take
ANIMAL ADJECTIVE
care of. I was told that all you have to do is feed her _____,
TYPE OF FOOD
make sure there's enough water in her _____, and
TYPE OF CONTAINER
_____ with her once in a while. Sounds _____, right?
VERB ADJECTIVE
Wrong! _____! That animal is so _____! It all
EXCLAMATION ADJECTIVE
started when I got on the school _____ to go home. She
VEHICLE
started _____ in her cage like a wild _____.
VERB ENDING IN "ING" SOMETHING ALIVE
Then, when I got her home, she escaped from her _____ and
NOUN
ran straight toward (the) _____. I tried to find her, but she
A PLACE
wasn't anywhere in our _____. _____, I still don't
TYPE OF BUILDING ADVERB
know where _____ is! Good thing it's snowing out. If
SAME SILLY WORD
we're off from school tomorrow, I'll have one more _____ to
NOUN
find her.

MAD LIBS® is fun to play with friends, but you can also play it by yourself! To begin with, DO NOT look at the story on the page below. Fill in the blanks on this page with the words called for. Then, using the words you have selected, fill in the blank spaces in the story.

Now you've created your own hilarious MAD LIBS® game!

CRAFTY PANTS

PLURAL NOUN _____

PLURAL NOUN _____

ANIMAL _____

TYPE OF FOOD _____

ADJECTIVE _____

VERB _____

NOUN _____

ADJECTIVE _____

VERB ENDING IN "ING" _____

TYPE OF LIQUID _____

VERB _____

ADJECTIVE _____

NOUN _____

ADJECTIVE _____

VERB _____

NOUN _____

ADJECTIVE _____

ADJECTIVE _____

MAD LIBS

CRAFTY PANTS

When I'm not in school, I like to get crafty with _____
                                                    PLURAL NOUN

I find around the house. Here are a few of my favorite arts and crafts

projects:

1. You can use leftover _____ to make a/an
                          PLURAL NOUN

    _____-house to hang outside and fill with bird-
       ANIMAL

    _____.
      TYPE OF FOOD

2. Making jewelry is always _____. _____
                               ADJECTIVE   VERB

    some macaroni onto a long _____ to make a/an
                                   NOUN

    _____ necklace.
        ADJECTIVE

3. Making slime is fun. You'll just need glue, _____
                                                 VERB ENDING IN "ING"

    soda, and a few drops of _____. _____ it all
                              TYPE OF LIQUID   VERB

    together until it's squishy and _____.
                                        ADJECTIVE

4. _____ tape is _____ and can be used to
          NOUN   ADJECTIVE

    _____ all kinds of things, like a/an _____ bag or
         VERB   NOUN

    a really _____ wallet. The possibilities are _____.
              ADJECTIVE   ADJECTIVE

From HOME FROM SCHOOL MAD LIBS® • Copyright © 2021 by Penguin Random House LLC

MAD LIBS® is fun to play with friends, but you can also play it by yourself! To begin with, DO NOT look at the story on the page below. Fill in the blanks on this page with the words called for. Then, using the words you have selected, fill in the blank spaces in the story.

Now you've created your own hilarious MAD LIBS® game!

FOR THE GOLD

NUMBER _____

VERB ENDING IN "ING" _____

ADJECTIVE _____

VERB ENDING IN "ING" _____

VERB _____

NOUN _____

VERB _____

VERB _____

TYPE OF FOOD _____

TYPE OF CONTAINER (PLURAL) _____

ADVERB _____

ANIMAL _____

PLURAL NOUN _____

ADJECTIVE _____

NOUN _____

PLURAL NOUN _____

VERB _____

MAD LIBS®

FOR THE GOLD

It's been snowing for _____ hours with no sign of
NUMBER

_____, but I refuse to let the weather make me
VERB ENDING IN "ING"

_____. I'm setting up a world-class obstacle course in my
ADJECTIVE

_____ room! The first thing you have to do is
VERB ENDING IN "ING"

_____ across the room carrying a/an _____ on a
VERB   NOUN

spoon. If you _____ it, you have to start again. Next, you
VERB

have to _____ over hot lava. But don't worry—the lava
VERB

is only a gallon of red _____ juice in a bunch of salad
TYPE OF FOOD

_____. Once you've _____
TYPE OF CONTAINER (PLURAL)   ADVERB

made it over the lava, you slither like a/an _____ under a
ANIMAL

tunnel of chairs. At the end of the tunnel, there's a mountain of stuffed

_____ that you have to climb over while singing "Twinkle,
PLURAL NOUN

Twinkle, _____ Star." Lastly, you have to get through a/an
ADJECTIVE

_____-field of pillows without getting hit by the cotton
NOUN

_____ my mother throws your way. It's the type of fun
PLURAL NOUN

the whole family can _____!
VERB

MAD LIBS® is fun to play with friends, but you can also play it by yourself! To begin with, DO NOT look at the story on the page below. Fill in the blanks on this page with the words called for. Then, using the words you have selected, fill in the blank spaces in the story.

Now you've created your own hilarious MAD LIBS® game!

STAY-AT-HOME SCHOOL

EXCLAMATION _____

VERB ENDING IN "ING" _____

ADJECTIVE _____

SILLY WORD _____

PART OF THE BODY (PLURAL) _____

ADJECTIVE _____

VERB _____

VERB _____

ANIMAL _____

VERB (PAST TENSE) _____

VERB ENDING IN "ING" _____

PART OF THE BODY _____

ADVERB _____

SAME ANIMAL _____

VERB ENDING IN "ING" _____

COUNTRY _____

NOUN _____

ADJECTIVE _____

MAD LIBS

STAY-AT-HOME SCHOOL

_____! We had school from home today! When that
EXCLAMATION

happens, it's called remote _____ and it's pretty
VERB ENDING IN "ING"

_____. We use a special computer program called
ADJECTIVE

_____, so all our _____ show up in
SILLY WORD   PART OF THE BODY (PLURAL)

_____ boxes on the screen. It's nice to _____ all my
ADJECTIVE   VERB

friends. Today, my math teacher was showing us how to _____
VERB

fractions when her pet _____ _____ on her
ANIMAL   VERB (PAST TENSE)

lap. It kept _____ the camera with its _____
VERB ENDING IN "ING"   PART OF THE BODY

while purring _____. And no matter how many times
ADVERB

our teacher put her _____ on the ground, it kept
SAME ANIMAL

_____ on her desk! While this was happening, one of
VERB ENDING IN "ING"

my friends kept changing his background to make it look like he was

sitting in _____, and someone else kept messaging the
COUNTRY

word "_____" on the group chat. It was the best math class
NOUN

ever—even if our teacher looked super _____ when it was
ADJECTIVE

over!

MAD LIBS® is fun to play with friends, but you can also play it by yourself! To begin with, DO NOT look at the story on the page below. Fill in the blanks on this page with the words called for. Then, using the words you have selected, fill in the blank spaces in the story.

Now you've created your own hilarious MAD LIBS® game!

ODE TO SNOW

VERB (PAST TENSE) _____

VERB (PAST TENSE) _____

ADJECTIVE _____

NOUN _____

OCCUPATION _____

VERB (PAST TENSE) _____

ADJECTIVE _____

ARTICLE OF CLOTHING (PLURAL) _____

ADJECTIVE _____

COLOR _____

PLURAL NOUN _____

NOUN _____

ADJECTIVE _____

VERB ENDING IN "ING" _____

MAD LIBS

ODE TO SNOW

Before I _____ to school today,
VERB (PAST TENSE)

I _____ up my coat.
VERB (PAST TENSE)

But then I felt a/an _____ snowy wind,
ADJECTIVE

on which many _____-flakes did float.
NOUN

My _____ said, "School's canceled."
OCCUPATION

So I _____ to find my sled.
VERB (PAST TENSE)

I put on my _____ _____
ADJECTIVE   ARTICLE OF CLOTHING (PLURAL)

and my _____ gloves that were _____ and red.
ADJECTIVE   COLOR

Outside, all my best _____ were lined up
PLURAL NOUN

on top of the steep _____ in long rows.
NOUN

They had the same _____ idea as me:
ADJECTIVE

to go _____ while it snows!
VERB ENDING IN "ING"

MAD LIBS® is fun to play with friends, but you can also play it by yourself! To begin with, DO NOT look at the story on the page below. Fill in the blanks on this page with the words called for. Then, using the words you have selected, fill in the blank spaces in the story.

Now you've created your own hilarious MAD LIBS® game!

GLAMPING

ADJECTIVE _____

TYPE OF BUILDING _____

VERB ENDING IN "ING" _____

VERB _____

NOUN _____

NOUN _____

NUMBER _____

VERB (PAST TENSE) _____

NOUN _____

EXCLAMATION _____

ADJECTIVE _____

VERB ENDING IN "ING" _____

ADJECTIVE _____

TYPE OF FOOD (PLURAL) _____

VERB ENDING IN "ING" _____

ADJECTIVE _____

VERB _____

ANIMAL (PLURAL) _____

MAD LIBS

GLAMPING

If it's snowing and you can't head to the _____

ADJECTIVE

outdoors, why not try indoor camping! First, find a good place in your

_____ to set up camp, like the _____ room.

TYPE OF BUILDING ⟶ VERB ENDING IN "ING"

Once you have a location, it's time to _____ up your shelter.

VERB

It's okay if you don't have a camping _____ because a few

NOUN

_____ chairs with _____ blankets _____

NOUN ⟶ NUMBER ⟶ VERB (PAST TENSE)

over them will do the trick. Next, roll out your sleeping _____

NOUN

and pillow, and _____! Now you have a/an _____

EXCLAMATION ⟶ ADJECTIVE

shelter! And all that _____ will probably make you

VERB ENDING IN "ING"

_____. This is a good time to pretend-roast hot

ADJECTIVE

_____ while _____ campfire songs on

TYPE OF FOOD (PLURAL) ⟶ VERB ENDING IN "ING"

your guitar or telling _____ ghost stories. It's a great way to

ADJECTIVE

_____ the day indoors, and the best part is, you don't have to

VERB

worry about _____ trying to get into your tent!

ANIMAL (PLURAL)

MAD LIBS® is fun to play with friends, but you can also play it by yourself! To begin with, DO NOT look at the story on the page below. Fill in the blanks on this page with the words called for. Then, using the words you have selected, fill in the blank spaces in the story.

Now you've created your own hilarious MAD LIBS® game!

THE QUIET GAME

CELEBRITY _____

ADJECTIVE _____

VERB ENDING IN "ING" _____

TYPE OF FOOD _____

VERB _____

ADJECTIVE _____

NOUN _____

SAME CELEBRITY _____

PLURAL NOUN _____

ADJECTIVE _____

NUMBER _____

PLURAL NOUN _____

VERB ENDING IN "ING" _____

PART OF THE BODY (PLURAL) _____

VERB ENDING IN "ING" _____

ANIMAL (PLURAL) _____

VERB ENDING IN "ING" _____

EXCLAMATION _____

MAD LIBS®

THE QUIET GAME

_____ and I are home from school today. I guess we were
CELEBRITY

being too loud because our mom asked us to try spending an hour

being totally _____ . No talking, no whispering, not even any
ADJECTIVE

_____ . At first, I thought it would be a piece of
VERB ENDING IN "ING"

_____ . I mean, all we had to do was just _____ and
TYPE OF FOOD   VERB

be _____ . I read an entire _____ while
   ADJECTIVE   NOUN

_____ flipped through some comic _____ .
SAME CELEBRITY   PLURAL NOUN

But then something _____ happened. Not being able to talk
                    ADJECTIVE

for _____ minutes gave us a bad case of the _____ .
    NUMBER   PLURAL NOUN

We just could not stop _____ . We put our
                        VERB ENDING IN "ING"

_____ over our mouths, but that didn't help. We
PART OF THE BODY (PLURAL)

even tried to stop laughing by not _____ at
                                    VERB ENDING IN "ING"

each other. But every time we did, we laughed like a pair of wild

_____ . Apparently, _____ quiet for an
ANIMAL (PLURAL)   VERB ENDING IN "ING"

hour was harder than we thought. _____ !
                                   EXCLAMATION

MAD LIBS® is fun to play with friends, but you can also play it by yourself! To begin with, DO NOT look at the story on the page below. Fill in the blanks on this page with the words called for. Then, using the words you have selected, fill in the blank spaces in the story.

Now you've created your own hilarious MAD LIBS® game!

LETTER TO GRANDMA

PERSON IN ROOM _____

VERB _____

ADJECTIVE _____

COUNTRY _____

ADJECTIVE _____

VERB _____

ADJECTIVE _____

TYPE OF FOOD _____

NUMBER _____

PLURAL NOUN _____

ADJECTIVE _____

VERB _____

VERB _____

NOUN _____

VERB _____

NOUN _____

CELEBRITY _____

MAD LIBS®

LETTER TO GRANDMA

Dear Grandma _____ ,
PERSON IN ROOM

Hi! Long time no _____ ! I'm home from school today so I
VERB

thought I'd write you a/an _____ letter. I hope the weather in
ADJECTIVE

_____ is _____ . What kind of food did you
COUNTRY   ADJECTIVE

_____ for lunch? Remember when we went to that
VERB

_____ restaurant together, and I ordered the baked
ADJECTIVE

_____ ? Then we went to the mall and looked in _____
TYPE OF FOOD   NUMBER

different stores to find you some rain _____ . We always
PLURAL NOUN

have a/an _____ time together! I wish you were here so you
ADJECTIVE

could _____ over and visit. Then, we could _____
VERB   VERB

together and I wouldn't have to use one of my rare _____
NOUN

stamps. I miss you and can't wait to _____ you!
VERB

Your grand- _____ ,
NOUN

_____
CELEBRITY

MAD LIBS® is fun to play with friends, but you can also play it by yourself! To begin with, DO NOT look at the story on the page below. Fill in the blanks on this page with the words called for. Then, using the words you have selected, fill in the blank spaces in the story.

Now you've created your own hilarious MAD LIBS® game!

SNOW-DAY COOKIES

VERB ENDING IN "ING" _____

VERB _____

NOUN _____

NUMBER _____

VERB _____

SOMETHING ALIVE _____

TYPE OF FOOD _____

COLOR _____

VERB _____

PART OF THE BODY _____

VERB _____

NOUN _____

PLURAL NOUN _____

NUMBER _____

PLURAL NOUN _____

VERB ENDING IN "ING" _____

MAD LIBS®

SNOW-DAY COOKIES

When I'm home from school on a snow day, I love _____
_____
VERB ENDING IN "ING"

healthy cookies. It's my secret recipe, so don't _____ it with
_____
VERB

anyone. First, take out your big mixing _____ . Then, dump
_____
NOUN

in _____ cups of almond flour and _____ it with a
_____   _____
NUMBER   VERB

tablespoon of baking soda and one teaspoon of _____
_____
SOMETHING ALIVE

sugar. Then add eight tablespoons of _____ . Next you will
_____
TYPE OF FOOD

need two _____ eggs. Be sure to _____ them
_____   _____
COLOR   VERB

carefully so you don't get any shells in the bowl. Otherwise, you might

end up chipping a/an _____ . Finally, _____ in the
_____   _____
PART OF THE BODY   VERB

best ingredient of all: the _____ chips! Once the ingredients
_____
NOUN

are all mixed together, form the dough into little _____
_____
PLURAL NOUN

and place them _____ inches apart on the baking sheet.
_____
NUMBER

Bake for about twelve minutes or until the kitchen smells like

_____ . Good luck not _____ them all
_____   _____
PLURAL NOUN   VERB ENDING IN "ING"

at once!

MAD LIBS® is fun to play with friends, but you can also play it by yourself! To begin with, DO NOT look at the story on the page below. Fill in the blanks on this page with the words called for. Then, using the words you have selected, fill in the blank spaces in the story.

Now you've created your own hilarious MAD LIBS® game!

GOING VIRAL

SILLY WORD _____

SILLY WORD _____

OCCUPATION (PLURAL) _____

PLURAL NOUN _____

NUMBER _____

VERB (PAST TENSE) _____

VERB ENDING IN "ING" _____

ADJECTIVE _____

NOUN _____

VERB _____

PART OF THE BODY _____

NOUN _____

PLURAL NOUN _____

VERB _____

PLURAL NOUN _____

NOUN _____

VERB _____

MAD LIBS

GOING VIRAL

Today, we didn't have school, so I asked my dad if I could make a/an

_____ - _____ video to show my _____
SILLY WORD   SILLY WORD   OCCUPATION (PLURAL)

how much I missed them. First, I watched a bunch of videos made by

other _____ to get some ideas. Next thing I knew,
PLURAL NOUN

_____ minutes had _____ by! It was time to start
NUMBER   VERB (PAST TENSE)

_____! I decided to put all our _____ pictures
VERB ENDING IN "ING"   ADJECTIVE

in the video and picked a beautiful piano _____ to go with
NOUN

the images. It almost made me _____ and will definitely tug
VERB

at my friends' _____ -strings. I even read a/an
PART OF THE BODY

_____ I wrote, titled: "Best _____ Forever No
NOUN   PLURAL NOUN

Matter What the Weather." Now all I have to do is _____ the
VERB

video and wait for the _____ to start rolling in! Please
PLURAL NOUN

smash that _____ button and _____ me if you like
NOUN   VERB

the video!

From HOME FROM SCHOOL MAD LIBS® • Copyright © 2021 by Penguin Random House LLC

MAD LIBS® is fun to play with friends, but you can also play it by yourself! To begin with, DO NOT look at the story on the page below. Fill in the blanks on this page with the words called for. Then, using the words you have selected, fill in the blank spaces in the story.

Now you've created your own hilarious MAD LIBS® game!

SPIN CYCLE

ADJECTIVE _____

VERB ENDING IN "ING" _____

PLURAL NOUN _____

VERB ENDING IN "ING" _____

TYPE OF CONTAINER _____

VERB _____

NOUN _____

VERB ENDING IN "ING" _____

TYPE OF FOOD _____

VERB _____

NOUN _____

ADVERB _____

VERB _____

NOUN _____

TYPE OF CONTAINER _____

EXCLAMATION _____

ADJECTIVE _____

ADJECTIVE _____

MAD LIBS®

SPIN CYCLE

You might think this is a little _____ , but I love doing my

ADJECTIVE

chores. Being home from school is a perfect time to catch up on

_____ my room. There's always a pile of dirty

VERB ENDING IN "ING"

_____ _____ next to my bed, which I have

PLURAL NOUN VERB ENDING IN "ING"

to put in my laundry _____ . It's relaxing to watch the

TYPE OF CONTAINER

clothes _____ in the washing _____ , and I love

VERB NOUN

fluffing and _____! Also, our soap is very bubbly and

VERB ENDING IN "ING"

smells like _____ . Then, I _____ back upstairs to

TYPE OF FOOD VERB

my room to organize my _____collection. When my room is

NOUN

_____ clean, I _____ to the kitchen for the broom

ADVERB VERB

because there's nothing better than sweeping the _____ . . .

NOUN

except putting new bags in the trash _____ .

TYPE OF CONTAINER

_____! Finally, everything is in order and I feel

EXCLAMATION

_____ . As my mother always says, "Clean room,

ADJECTIVE

_____ mind!"

ADJECTIVE

MAD LIBS® is fun to play with friends, but you can also play it by yourself! To begin with, DO NOT look at the story on the page below. Fill in the blanks on this page with the words called for. Then, using the words you have selected, fill in the blank spaces in the story.

Now you've created your own hilarious MAD LIBS® game!

NAP TIME

ADJECTIVE _____

ADVERB _____

ADJECTIVE _____

VERB _____

VERB _____

PART OF THE BODY _____

VERB _____

ADJECTIVE _____

ANIMAL _____

NUMBER _____

PERSON IN ROOM _____

VERB _____

VERB _____

VERB ENDING IN "ING" _____

PLURAL NOUN _____

EXCLAMATION _____

ADJECTIVE _____

MAD LIBS

NAP TIME

One of the best things about having a snow day is taking a nice,

_____ nap. Here's how to sleep _____ during the
   ADJECTIVE   ADVERB

day:

1. This might sound _____, but it helps to make your bed
                          ADJECTIVE

    before you _____ back in it. _____ all
             VERB   VERB

    your pillows and get your _____-buds ready to
                       PART OF THE BODY

    _____ to some _____ music.
       VERB   ADJECTIVE

2. Make sure your stuffed _____ is on the bed. I've had
                     ANIMAL

    mine for _____ years and she helps me sleep. Her name is
           NUMBER

    Lady Snuggle _____.
          PERSON IN ROOM

3. Finally, _____ off the light and _____
           VERB   VERB

    into bed—and without _____ on those
                   VERB ENDING IN "ING"

    _____ you left on the floor! _____! Getting
     PLURAL NOUN   EXCLAMATION

    ready for a nap is _____.
              ADJECTIVE

MAD LIBS® is fun to play with friends, but you can also play it by yourself! To begin with, DO NOT look at the story on the page below. Fill in the blanks on this page with the words called for. Then, using the words you have selected, fill in the blank spaces in the story.

Now you've created your own hilarious MAD LIBS® game!

SNOW DAY, YES WAY!

NOUN _____

ADJECTIVE _____

VERB _____

ARTICLE OF CLOTHING _____

ADJECTIVE _____

VERB ENDING IN "ING" _____

OCCUPATION (PLURAL) _____

NOUN _____

VERB _____

ADJECTIVE _____

EXCLAMATION _____

SILLY WORD _____

VERB _____

VERB _____

SOMETHING ALIVE _____

ADJECTIVE _____

TYPE OF LIQUID _____

VERB _____

MAD LIBS®

SNOW DAY, YES WAY!

It's a/an _____ day! There are so many _____ things
            NOUN   ADJECTIVE

to do, I don't even know where to _____. Of course, you have
                                        VERB

to make sure to wear your hat and _____ when
                                       ARTICLE OF CLOTHING

you go outside. You don't want to be too _____ when
                                               ADJECTIVE

_____ in the snow all day. Especially if you're making
VERB ENDING IN "ING"

snow- _____ or if you get into a/an _____ -ball
       OCCUPATION (PLURAL)   NOUN

fight with your little sister. Another activity I really like is sledding. I

_____ my sled all the way up the _____ hill in my
     VERB   ADJECTIVE

backyard, then off I go. _____! My sled is a Super-Duper
                             EXCLAMATION

_____ , which goes really fast. I always make sure to
    SILLY WORD

_____ off at just the right time so I don't _____ into
     VERB   VERB

the _____ at the bottom of the hill. After an hour of
       SOMETHING ALIVE

sledding, I get _____ , so I usually go inside for a nice cup of
                   ADJECTIVE

hot _____ . It's a perfect way to _____ the day,
      TYPE OF LIQUID   VERB

don't you think?

MAD LIBS® is fun to play with friends, but you can also play it by yourself! To begin with, DO NOT look at the story on the page below. Fill in the blanks on this page with the words called for. Then, using the words you have selected, fill in the blank spaces in the story.

Now you've created your own hilarious MAD LIBS® game!

GAME TIME

VERB ENDING IN "ING" _____

NUMBER _____

VERB _____

ADJECTIVE _____

NOUN _____

VERB ENDING IN "ING" _____

PART OF THE BODY _____

FIRST NAME _____

ADJECTIVE _____

NUMBER _____

PART OF THE BODY _____

SILLY WORD _____

PLURAL NOUN _____

VERB ENDING IN "ING" _____

PLURAL NOUN _____

ADJECTIVE _____

VERB _____

NOUN _____

MAD LIBS

GAME TIME

I've been _____ all day for my _____ minutes of
      VERB ENDING IN "ING"   NUMBER

screen time, and it's finally here! How should I _____ it? I
              VERB

really love playing _____ video games. Right now, I'm into
         ADJECTIVE

_____-*craft*. I love building and _____ new
  NOUN   VERB ENDING IN "ING"

worlds. On the other _____, I also enjoy playing *The*
         PART OF THE BODY

Legend of _____. Once, when I was playing _____
      FIRST NAME   ADJECTIVE

Mario Bros., I played for _____ hours straight! That theme song
          NUMBER

was stuck in my _____ for weeks. _____! There
      PART OF THE BODY   SILLY WORD

are so many new _____ to choose from and my time is
        PLURAL NOUN

_____ out! And I still didn't get to download the new
  VERB ENDING IN "ING"

Star _____ game yet. I know one thing is _____:
     PLURAL NOUN   ADJECTIVE

If I don't _____ soon, I'll never get to play any games, and I'll
      VERB

end up staring at this blank _____ instead of having any fun!
          NOUN

MAD LIBS® is fun to play with friends, but you can also play it by yourself! To begin with, DO NOT look at the story on the page below. Fill in the blanks on this page with the words called for. Then, using the words you have selected, fill in the blank spaces in the story.

Now you've created your own hilarious MAD LIBS® game!

BOREDOM BUSTERS

NOUN _____

ADJECTIVE _____

ANIMAL _____

PLURAL NOUN _____

VERB _____

PART OF THE BODY (PLURAL) _____

VERB _____

ARTICLE OF CLOTHING (PLURAL) _____

NOUN _____

NUMBER _____

NOUN _____

TYPE OF LIQUID _____

EXCLAMATION _____

VERB ENDING IN "ING" _____

NOUN _____

NOUN _____

VERB _____

VERB (PAST TENSE) _____

MAD LIBS

BOREDOM BUSTERS

Stuck indoors? Try these _____ busters!
NOUN

1. Teach your _____ _____ some new
ADJECTIVE   ANIMAL

_____! Can they sit? _____ down? Shake
PLURAL NOUN   VERB

_____?
PART OF THE BODY (PLURAL)

2. Self-portraits can be fun. _____ up in layers of
VERB

_____, sit on a/an _____,
ARTICLE OF CLOTHING (PLURAL)   NOUN

and take _____ photographs.
NUMBER

3. Take a hot _____ bath. While the water is running, pour
NOUN

in a cup of _____ . . . and _____! Your
TYPE OF LIQUID   EXCLAMATION

bubble bath is ready—happy _____!
VERB ENDING IN "ING"

4. Write yourself a/an _____. Sign your _____ at
NOUN   NOUN

the bottom of the letter, and _____ it in the mail.
VERB

By the time it comes back to you, you'll have forgotten everything

you _____!
VERB (PAST TENSE)